THE SALT OF MY TEARS

LATONYA STEPHENS, PHD
Uncapped Inspiration from the Philosopher of Life & Marriage

Copyright © 2022 by Latonya Stephens, PhD

The Salt of My Tears

All rights reserved. No part of this publication may be reproduced, stored in a retrieval system, or transmitted in any form or by any means, electronic, mechanical, photocopying, recording or otherwise without the prior permission of the publisher or in accordance with the provisions of the Copyright, Designs and Patents Act 1988 or under the terms of any license permitting limited copying issued by the Copyright Licensing Agency.

Cover photo credit: Robyn Lowe

Illustration credit: Jaslyn Love

Copyedit by: Joy Wilson

For speaking engagements and book signing email: uncappedinspiration@gmail.com

Uncapped Inspiration
Attn: Latonya Stephens, PhD
P.O. Box 35084
Kansas City, MO 64030

Dedications

The following poems are dedicated to every person who is finding their voice and wrestling with grief. May every tear shed wash away the pain of your past and nurture new life.

Special thanks to Monique Lisa, who can effectively pull a harvest from a seed. You are amazing!

Thank you, Pastor J, (from The House of Creativity), for investing in a stranger with faith in what God can do!

Thank you, hubby, for your patience and son for joining me in my writing journey.

In memory of Ruby

FOREWORD

BY
DEBORAH PEGUES

Poetry is an international language. It connects and gives voice to individuals globally. The voice of **The Salt of My Tears** is intentionally bold, honest, and uncapped. When we think of salt, we typically think of seasoning for food. But life is a lot like salt. They are both experienced in multiple ways. If you allow yourself to fully taste it, it can be a healing agent as you evolve, or you can abuse it and experience harm.

Latonya's invitation on this poetic journey provides a space for healing and a better you. Each tear you shed will free you from burdens, insecurity, pain, and grief. This book provides insight, wisdom, and a literary sister-friend.

You will experience tears of grief and tears of joy, pain, and hope.

I identify with a part of Latonya's journey because we shared the loss of our mutual friend, Ruby. I have had my share of joys and sorrows. I have experienced disappointment, rejection, discrimination, health challenges, and adversities on several fronts, notwithstanding, I have also experienced victories, the true love of a husband for over four decades, good friends, and the favor of God. It's called life.

I am grateful that Latonya did not resort to "speaking like a weakling" in this body of work but allowed herself to become "vulnerable". I am so proud of her. As a mentee, she listened. As a woman, she fought for destiny. As a lady, she allowed herself to experience life and now shares it with you.

When I read **The Salt of My Tears,** I felt life in 3D. It reminded me that trials are temporary. It also reminded me that you can take the salt of life and allow it to either season you or ruin you. What you do with salt and how you use it can determine your physical outcome.

How you manage life can determine how you live life, bitter or whole. Let's take the journey of life together and allow it to season us with grace.

Sister-friend, find your place of comfort, put on your favorite pajamas, and grab your favorite drink. Together, we are going to allow poetry to awaken our soul for healing and experience a "New Baptism" of joy and love. Welcome to the **Salt of My Tears**.

The Table of Contents

Foreword	6
The Salt of my Tears	10
Where the Caterpillars Perch	17
Plums to Prunes	22
The Death of Complaints	27
The Sting of Death	34
When Death Dies	36
The Resurrection of Black	42
Under the Half Moon in Cancun	47
The Second Ruby	50
30,000 Feet	53
Broken Wings	56
Uncaged	58
Burning Birds	61
The Verdict	64
Bloody Dirt	67
Dear God	70
Greed	72
The Get Up Swing	76
That New Baptism	78
Author's Note	104

THE FIRST TEAR
THE SALT OF MY TEARS

I've waited to taste the flavor of your love
    seasoned with friendship
        grace, and adventure
            But then, code blue, 5150
                a pulsating
                    lake of blood

My eyes swelled
    like a roaring wave
        when I heard a wail
            from the bottom of
                my soul

In that moment
    life felt like death
        Death never felt like life
            It instantly left me cold

Life brings so many experiences
Some good and some bad

Good, because there was an opportunity
to taste it
Bad, because life also made me sad

Life can be spicy, sweet, cool, hot
or draining, heated and dry
I looked at life and it appeared sweet
until I tasted it
it was tart and made me cry

I saw life become sour, like a salted lemon
that created a rotting black hole
Although it felt like my soul deteriorated, it
was good for me, but hard to console

You see, Monday, I cried
Until I tasted salt from my eyes

I tasted the nutrient of pain and deceit
I tasted suffering like a boxer getting beat

I fell through the ropes
that were dry and rough
This part of life was full of tough stuff

I tasted the hurt, the tribulation, and trials
It reminded me to walk the extra mile

Grainy Salt

Too much pain brings a sour taste, bitterness, isolation and questions
Too much sadness breeds anxiety, fear, and rough lessons

Pure Salt

But why not sugar from the eyes of the experienced?
Why not sugar from the eyes of the loved?

Coarse Salt

Like a scar, the experience from the pain of
death marked my soul
and unknowingly, I craved it again, leaving
that deep jagged hole

Leaving a void, watery eyes out of control
testifying of stories untold

Dirty tears from chemicals imbalanced
They seemed flavorful, but left me
challenged

Dry Salt

I looked and saw breaths
staggering in and out
Daunted, but hope yet remained.

Until I saw the perfect beauty of love
On the face that was yet unstained

Surrounded by others
adding their flat-lined hope
I became frustrated by the absence of sound

Surrounded by silence, it added pressure
feeling like anxiety-go-round

I tasted salt before
but this time it was different

It was more liquified than dry
It welled up and dripped
from my cheek it slipped
until I felt salt fall
from my eye

Each tear drop connected
and flowed like a river
cleaning rocks on a downward slope

Then I thought of the flavor
that was added to my life
I chuckled. They were right! I can cope!

Liquid Salt

It's a healing agent
It stings, scrubbing the wounds of my past
Yes, it was painful. It refined my heart
but I'm left with a love that lasts

The salt cleansed me
    of negativity
        as I watched my friend go free

Embracing memories
    that is now her-story
        my memory will forever be...

Perfectly Salt

The pages of my heart flipped to a time
when the voice of experience
consoled my mind

It was the right ingredient of words
I will never forget
mixed to keep me from the pain of regret

You see food without salt
is like life without being taught
By someone who brings clarity
erasing fears

I'm all choked up
by the salt of this bitter cup
Tears flow
and again, I taste the salt of my tears

THE SECOND TEAR
WHERE THE CATERPILLARS PERCH

The cycle of life can feel complicated
in the soul of man
We are birthed to serve purpose
until the end of our life span

Leaving questions unanswered, leaving
potential in the grave
Despising death, but keep moving,
because it will misbehave

In the community, through the city,
through the nation and the church
It visited my space
where the caterpillars perch

Up, down, body moving
roaming through the grass of life
You and I, like the caterpillar
dodging predators, life's knife

Crawling through blades
of weed and dirt
searching for substance
but getting hurt

Ignorant of the space above
protecting my innocence, seeking Love

A quick glance into the sky
to see the colorful butterfly
Dodged a shoe and sticky fingers
the sight of awesomeness flew by

A field of green, can you see it?
It will feed me for the next 10 days

I am settled, but not complete
feeling heat from God's sun rays

A place of stillness, in a place alone
This lonely place is my new home

Days pass, sleep takes over
fighting the melt down
like poor luck from a clover

Now stuck and entrapped
but can't resist
The satisfaction of comfort
is this an abyss?

I fade. I wake up… vision blurred
feeling an urge
ready to surge

Movement needed
Hunger strikes
Movement's a must
Giving all my might

A breakthrough hits
There's something new
What, a wing! Something grew
I push to get out of this suffocating place
If I push hard enough
I'll have a breakthrough

There is life on the other side
I press through this space
I can't wait to see the other side
I'm leaving this place

I can't believe it! Is it me?
I see an image below
Who would have thought?
Hallelujah! I'm the hit of life's show

I remembered the greenery
and what life brought
I remembered the sharp lessons
those old weeds taught

I dodged a pit, I dodged a shoe
I dodged death, it came for me too

I melted, was dissolved
and restored at the church
I flew from the place
where the caterpillars perch

THE THIRD TEAR
PLUMS TO PRUNES

Take a deep breath. It won't last long
Here comes the next wave of heat

Inhale, exhale. Breathe slowly
The sun comes to make you complete

The heart sinks… I see you

I see the pain. I see the hurt
I saw you overwhelmed with dirt
Dust splattered like a party boy's flirt
With the nerve to serve you rudely and curt

Boogie down baby
Shake the dust off your back

I saw the darts
that were thrown to attack

To attack your heart, attack your soul
Nights of anguish, feeling out of control

The loss, the abuse
the abandonment, the crush
Anvils on the heart
the impressions to hush

Then a yell...

There's a sound from heaven
a breakthrough of light
Exposing the flaws
a change in the night

The voices you hear
confusing the soul

Should I stay
or should I go?

Don't lose control

Take the reins on life
steering with your might
Rescuing from darkness
no enemies in sight

The enemies of the soul
insecurity, and fear
Pressing from darkness
God's voice so clear

Ya gotta keep your head up
Embracing that amazing grace
Kicking your butt from pity and shame
Until you see the sun on your face

No more darkness
death still comes
but beauty springs from the cocoon
Darkness attracting Light
redirecting your fight
shrinking dark plums into prunes

Life is like prunes and meant to be
experienced
But growing old never seems to cease
It kisses death, but brings new life
Enduring sun, trials, and heat

Yielding to age, and a bright future
but wisdom shows a wrinkled face
Your beauty never faded, it only changed
to deliver a promising grace

So, experience life, it sharpens character
to produce the best in you
Like plums to prunes, get sweeter with
time
but stay away from strange fruit

THE FOURTH TEAR
THE DEATH OF COMPLAINTS

Pull your own weight
so, you will know how it feels
Carrying loads of mental freight
was never part of the deal

The ball came to my court
and again, I was taken for-granted
Heart shaded like a bad diss in public
while my soul panted

From the embarrassment of harsh words
but I took it like a champ
Only to recognize selfishness
and for my lips to be clamped

For someone to understand
and work with me as a team
To look proudly in your eyes
and swell with gleam

It was your responsibility
and then it became ours
I took on responsibility
I worked it for hours

The hours became days
the days became years
You said that you had me
now I only experience tears

The tears from complaints
of what I did wrong
Not facing my fears
but hearing the same old song

Straighten your curly hair
Change your boring clothes
How about a hat?
What's next, alter my nose?

Why do you clean like that?
What are you putting in the food?

Why do you need to do that?
There were so many rules

I saw through the lies
I saw through the game
I was tired of the harsh voice
I left with a choice

What's your issue?
What's your problem?
That's all that I heard

I'd run away in my mind
like a fed up, angry bird

It felt like a tragedy
striking on a gloomy day
Like an immoveable weight
after a sacrifice, I'd say

My brain felt full
and overwhelmed with much grief
Looking for a listening ear
trying to find quick relief

After running here
and walking there
Hula hooping
and climbing stairs

from Zumba to Zoom
and back to my room

Looking to cope
but only ending with gloom

The noise had to stop
like an ending to a storm
Another death and food shortage
is this now the new norm?

You're doing too much!
Can you cook today?
Nothing's in the kitchen!
Can I have it my way?

It's hot! I'm sweaty!
I really need to rest

Nature calls from willow trees
swaying east, moving west

Bringing shade
Calming me
Helping me breathe
buzzing bee...
In my ear
threatening to sting
Complaints diminishing
I'm doing my thing

Saying no
a good word for me
Soothing the heart
from negativity

Focused and still
not ready to move
The branches in the wind
are stirring my groove

I feel a warmth
rejuvenating the soul
Weights being lifted
an accomplished goal

I laughed from the stings
that attacked my back
Resting from the noise,
left on hell's death rack

THE FIFTH TEAR
THE STING OF DEATH

The Bible says
that the sting of death is sin
But I yet wrestle with five stings within

My flesh holds captive
the possibility of deceit
while hell hopes I yield
being swept off my feet

Resisting temptation
From the voice in my head
Doubters that say I'm already dead

Questioning my journey
Questioning my life
Questioning God
"Am I more than a wife?"

Resisting the lie that says I'm invisible
Resisting the pressure
Resisting the crucible

Drunkenness came, drunkenness went
Without a care, my actions were hell bent

But grace said freedom
my heart failing within
I stumbled over truth
Ignorance shielded my sin

Until Love came
And rescued me from myself
Truth rescued me
From the stings of death

THE SIXTH TEAR
WHEN DEATH DIES

If death is the absence of life
Can we live until death ceases?
Fear robs the soul of love
killing relationships beginning with you

If death is the absence of life
Can we live until death subsides?
Depression robs the soul of joy
Destroying the heart like break-ups do

If death is the absence of life
Can we live until death ends?
Stress robs the soul of health
Diminishing cells, then anastasis

If death is the absence of life
Can we live until death ends
The peace I have, grants me new life
Death dies because I live again

THE SEVENTH TEAR
FRIENDSHIPS & FREEDOM

Freedom is a place
that embraces the sky
Released from hurt
where time goes by

Freedom is a place
Where time goes fast
Enjoying moments
Hoping forever they'd last

Freedom is a place
where no one can judge
because opinions never matter
where truth is indulged

Freedom is a place
where boundaries earn respect
protecting the heart
avoiding mental debt

Freedom is that place
where peace often dwells
Finding rest from the stress
that comes from bitter wells

Freedom is a place
that attracts the good and the bad
Captivating hungry souls
to the best experience ever had

Freedom is a place
that welcomes your everyday
Avoiding roads of distractions
that can lead you astray

Freedom is that place
Where you can leave all pain behind
No sorrow, no fear
Nor a captive of your own mind

Freedom is also that place
Where creativity
carves a new road and path
God's plan, your plan, you *is* smart
You do the math

Freedom is that place in life
where you spend borrowed time
Live life in abundance
don't worry, it's on God's dime

So, freedom is also a place
of responsibility
Lose one, win some
a thankful soul will be set free

So, win big with your selflessness
and that big, beautiful smile
Don't worry, that seed sown
will go for a million miles

And that's all it takes
to be truly free indeed
Only God in between
faithful you, faithful me

THE EIGHTH TEAR
THE RESURRECTION OF BLACK

Black by one definition
is the darkest color of the night
A disappearing adjective
often associated with fright

Let me give this all my might
providing an understanding
of what this means
A description in black and white
making it invisible
and as a person unseen

From the continent's coast
of a bright people, full of pride

I remember that dark space
where joy ceased and my spirit died

The process began
when my brother lied...
about who I was
to which my soul was tied

El tonto negro they said as they watched
bare brown feet pound the dirt

Der schwarze Narr deceiving the king
and on the people inflicted hurt

The effort to capture the identity of souls
and affiliate brown skin to black
Minimizing ethnicity
calling ignorant eccentricity
there were jewels they never gave back

The values of integrity, trust, and love
was out the window
once their heart devised to steal

The minerals and inventions
men and women from their habitation
in exchange for a bad deal

Negro and Narr was depicted as ignorant
Black was considered ugly
Black became the new name
for a people of stature
who now found themselves struggling

The greatest looking of the beauties
the most intellectual of the intelligent
only the strong survived

Snatched from their babies
heart fainted; men emasculated
for their evil brothers to thrive

Bitterness sold the community's warrior
strife pimped its sister
But the hero of salvation will come
and the froward will reap from The Mister

Down to the river to cleanse the stench
from the place of no return
Many died, but Black resurrected
with resilience, with envy they'll burn

With memories and regret
a generation will suffer
what the thief and the heartless stole

The law of reciprocity is not mine to dish
but you will reap what was sown

In the land meant to bury
the meaning of their name
only sprouts with new seed scattered
Arose from one of up to 500 million
who died and human cells splattered

In the dark of the night
through the hallow black tunnel
lent a light to a brighter day

The evil that formed
To destroy the strong
Only made them stronger they say

The brilliant will rise
in the land of deceit
that built the nation on their back
The crime projected onto the innocent
will return and resurrect the Black

THE NINTH TEAR
UNDER THE HALF MOON IN CANCUN

I was standing under the half-moon
in Cancun when I saw two stars
One shining east, one shining west
one shining orangish like Sherbert
like Mars

Feeling exhausted, like a mine worker
after a 16-hour shift
I walk like a sloth to my room
hitting the bed my mind drifts

I hear the roaring sound
of the ocean waves
beating against my small brown ear

It brought peace like a river
now shifting to relaxation
please don't wake me, my dear

The heat with the night sky
hypnotized me
and sent me into a deep meditation

I come alive, like a dead man left limp
at a noisy, inner-city train station

Behind my eyelids, no light seeping
through surely a change is going to come
Slipping deeper in the night, I finally rest
in Mexico, like a bum drunk from rum

Ten hours pass, revived from sleep
and now I am just simply tired
I wake up moving like a little turtle
to the masseuse to feel the warm fire

The heat from the sun
the heat from the hands
of a man I really don't know
I stayed as long as I could
begging for more with my body
but now I really must go

It's time to eat, but I'm starving for words
to wrap my mind and bring relief
I grab my digital companion and boom
I write about my process from grief

I share my heart until I'm done
and witness the shining half moon
I empty my soul like a bottle of tequila
dripping from a man in Cancun

THE TENTH TEAR
THE SECOND RUBY

Pink and purple were their colors
but lived two worlds apart

Both were spunky, one was childless
They shared a selfless heart

They shared the same name
but never met
Were posh, poised, and pristine

They loved to live, but fought for it
'til the end their hands were clean

Never perfect, but perfectly loved
There was none that was a stranger

You could eat at their table
eat on fine China
But they'd never
touch a cow in a manger

The first Ruby, biologically connected
Was the grandmother I never knew

The second Ruby
was spiritually connected
and was engraved into my heart too

Both I saw until the end
I felt their love t'was pure

Learning valuable lessons
from them both
Life til 100, I was so sure

The first Ruby instilled wisdom for life

For relationships, etiquette, and such

The second Ruby embodied

the spirit of loveliness

Her kindness I miss very much

I see the first Ruby in how I relate

and how I build my home

The second Ruby

enforced unconditional love

which birthed this book of poems

So, if you find a Ruby
Hold on to the gem inside
Your life will truly benefit
If within your heart they hide

THE ELEVENTH TEAR
30,000 FEET

30,000 feet above ground
and I can't come down
High in the sky
with no worries, no frowns

A hallelujah in my heart
from the songs, I drown
basking in your presence
eyes closed, twirling 'round

Doors open, doors closed
keeping me safe from the noise

Riding waves, conquering tides
with Jesus Christ I'll ride

Never flooded by the darkest fear
keeping the testimony
of the Word so near

To escape death like a cat with nine lives
Holy Spirit take the wheel and drive

Past the vibrations of negativity
Past the voices trying to taunt me

The higher we go, the vipers they fall
The chattering snakes
they will soon stonewall

30,000 feet and I won't come down
until Jesus comes
and cracks open the ground

Mother Earth with labor pains
making room for the dead
Her core opens, releasing me from my
captured soul's death bed

Not resisting the sound
I rise to a new beat 30,000 feet
I open my eyes, twas a dream
back to sleep, rewind, repeat

THE TWELFTH TEAR
BROKEN WINGS

I once had a bird named Charlie Blue
he chirped and flew around
He'd sing and eat, landing his gray beak
in his bowl of bird feed bound

In his cage all day and night
until I'd open the cage
Charlie would fly
returning to my shoulder
he brought such happy days

Then one day I left
leaving him in sister's care
She forgot to give him water

It was the hottest day
of the summer that year
I returned to a limped bird altered

He tried to fly but fell quickly
The heat had taken his breath
He tried to fly with broken wings
until I accepted his death

THE THIRTEENTH TEAR
UNCAGED

Surrounded by the ivory white
trapped inside like dynamite

Ready to explode, but encaged tight
Clinching teeth, my tongue must fight

To restore the life that I once knew
to rebuild my core, withdrawn from feuds

Death spoken over my essence
I shrank
words of death spoken, from that cup
I drank

Fear had shaken my core
from the response

Fear took hold of my tongue
feeling numb

Tuned out from the noise
that incited trauma
Needed a solution to eliminate the drama

In moments like these
I needed my momma
To remind me of the voice I had
now I'mma

Speak my heart and risk the retaliation
Speak my truth, speak without hesitation

I'mma be my full self
and not think about the rage
This day, I give love
my tongue loosed and uncaged

THE FOURTEENTH TEAR
BURNING BIRDS

Tell me, what is this world coming to?
A musical experience turned lawsuit

Massive crowds running forward to hear
The sound of burning birds in 7th gear

Thousands of souls, lungs gasping for air
As the heat increased
from the bird's vocal flare

Pressing forward to hear
the idol's vulgar words
the suffocation increased
cries for help unheard

The music gets louder
the screams overbearing

The traumatizing reality
of a few men caring

Another rush
pushes the crowd to a stampede
rockabye baby lights out, the birds bleed

Night owls wait
hoping the show will soon end
burning birds died
next to strangers and good friends

Help, I can't breathe
was the lyric of the night
the beat dropped, hearts stopped
now filled with fright

A new sound was heard
matching lights of white and red
young ears grew deaf
burning birds alone and dead

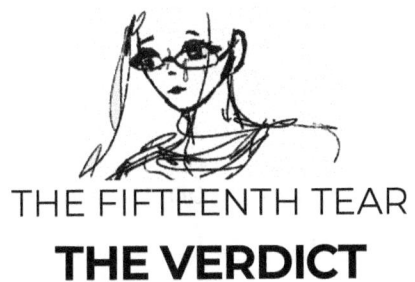

THE FIFTEENTH TEAR
THE VERDICT

Not guilty was the verdict
that cracked the television screen
In disbelief
knowing his dirty hands
were wiped clean

That smirk hidden behind
the breakdown of faulty tears
Don't worry, the truth will haunt
and taunt him for years

The shot that broke the vein to the heart
The verdict that ripped the nation apart

Further from the truth
Further from the start

From one nation, under God
the devil's eyes sparked

With destruction and deceit
filled with wickedness and pride
No consideration for the future
PTSD will take you on a ride

Visiting your grands
to the fifth generation
You're going to wish
you escaped this nation

The legacy you left
you're going to need a savior
To rescue you from yourself
you signed life's waiver

Welcoming a life sentence
not attentive to the penalties
Night terrors, visiting faces
desperately wanting to be free

Escaped jail from behind bars
and a death sentence I believe
That the verdict was a release
into the hands of the three

Innocent souls tormented
in seconds spirits released
The consequence of murder
is a guilty verdict in the streets

THE SIXTEENTH TEAR
BLOODY DIRT

Stop the hatred, the murder and lies
Aren't you tired of hearing brother cry?

Flaked to the earth
from the bones abhorred
The Earth groans from the pains of labor

Poked and prodded
like the king's stepdaughter
Braxton hicks
but it's too hard to soothe her

Stop the madness and pride that stinks
Identity stolen, but it's not what you think

A slain sister here
and wounded brother there

Too many bitter souls
who bears the tear

The heart of the mother
that wails in the night
Her back, in pain
and now throbbing and tight

That poor woman's soul
is wrestling with grief
Refusing to settle
for that fruitless green leaf

I'm Black, I'm Brown
I'm White, I'm Red
Crayons defined us
and now kids are dead

But the blood that we share
gives life to us all
We're just dirt, dusty dirt
I'm not "yo or y'all"

Who can pay the price
for the lives in Mother Earth?
A ransom for a people that was loyal

See we're prized of gold, copper,
and other fine things
The darker the dirt the richer the soil

So, the next time you plan
to shed innocent blood
Remember the price that you must pay

The bloody dirt cries to guilty ears why?
To remind them
of what was done that day

THE SEVENTEENTH TEAR
DEAR GOD

Dear God, I wrestle

I wrestle with the trauma
in the present from my past
Albeit it was yesterday
I wrestle not with unforgiveness
but to forget what just took place

How do you erase the stains on the soul
that torments day by day?

70x7 seems to not be enough
Because I still have to deal with this stuff

Time after time and time again
it becomes a mental frustration

It should be a sin

to repeat the same patterns

that lead to down-right manipulation

I have seconds of unforgiveness

then quickly forgive

Then the thoughts come back again

Dear God, deliver me from this match

before I lose my cool and sin

THE EIGHTEENTH TEAR
GREED

I watched the face of greed
from the screen
Inviting me to join the crowd

I politely declined
humiliated by the chatter
The noise was invoked and loud

My skin color was mocked
by the paid sponsors
in shirts of black and white

If pride could, it would parade itself
snatching power from what is right

How dare you claim American rights
To a country where you weren't invited

Depriving the natives
peacocking the thieves
The stolen were forced labor and slighted

The thief always steals
until theirs is stolen
Then cry and play the sad victim

A greedy man's food sits, slow to digest
It sits until a laxative hit him

The larger the belly
the lower the conscience
Of what someone else may need

To gratify your flesh
ignoring others for yourself
Our nation is filled with greed

Modesty is a foreign word
greed abuses boys and girls
The granny and papa must work

But ignorance
ignored the tragedy of death
Now the aging is disappearing
like job perks

Where's the beef, the chicken, and fish
The markets are low in supply

The hospitals are full, the polls are empty
They say the voting process must die

Sore losers never win
their honesty struggles
To claim the rights for others

Most fools stand alone

now obey that commandment

To not covet

what belongs to your brother

THE NINETEENTH TEAR
THE GET UP SWING

Hey girl, what are you doing
still laying in the bed
Get up! Get dressed
and put on your best red

Red lips, red shirt, red shoes, red hat
Ignite that fire, don't act like a brat

Hey girl, what are you doing
still moping around
It's time to dance, two-step
don't act like you're bound

Shake them hips left and right
Pop, lock, drop fingers pop

Rock that head move to the beat
Slide in socks, move them feet

Clap one, two cadence calls
Sing one hit, that is all

Get up Sis, one more time
I see you Sis in your prime

Love your swag, girl get down
See that smile… oooo no frowns

Get down girl, I'm inspired
I encouraged myself, this girl sparked fire

THE TWENTIETH TEAR
THAT NEW BAPTISM

The confessions from my soul were loud
Like a melting pot
boiled over into a crowd

Shouted to rid myself of the pain
I wrote emphatically like pouring rain

I betrayed myself and I had to deal with it
Like drinking dirty water and getting sick

It spewed back my tears until I
regurgitated
The words to my heart
where the seeds were planted

Seeds of doubt, failure, and negativity
Seeds scattered from the crowd
and back to me

Words of blasphemy, my name profaned
I was left feeling
naked, blamed, and ashamed

I crawled within, my tongue was tamed
I wanted to cuss; my heart said the same

The stare of pride is thick
now, who's the dame?
Pride's cruel like the grave
it plays no games

Baptized by salty tears
washing away the hurt
The reflection of beauty with
disappearing dirt

Sticks, stones and words chops
hurt and cuts
To the core, gotta heal
rebound and now what

To the pool of forgiveness
where the tears roll down
It's that new baptism
old waves, new sound

Listening through the ears of glee
No dirty words taunting me
Tears washed me clean, and now I'm free
It's that new baptism
that allows me to be

Like an eagle that soars
above the dark clouds
It's that new baptism
teary river, above ground

Backscattered rays that ignited my heart
Leaving behind the taunt
that pierced like darts

Immaturity in a world
that leads to ignorance
It's that new baptism
new thoughts, new chance

To experience life like a horse
and a swimming turtle
Racing strong, moving slow, fixed
and shaped like a girdle

It's that new baptism
that makes people most afraid
Head back, eyes closed
water flow, no rage

A cleaned heart, pure thoughts
now I'll do my part
Walked through valleys and caves
fresh tears, new start

It's that new baptism
that cleansed the soul
Fear blocked the pool ducts
that dripped stories untold

No sips from the spirits
of falsehood and rage
It's that new baptism
like a river with no cag

Dearest friend,

Please share lessons from times you have struggled to see and love yourself.

_____
_____
_____
_____
_____
_____
_____
_____
_____
_____
_____
_____
_____
_____
_____
_____
_____
_____
_____

The caterpillar doesn't understand the life
of the butterfly.
Because they have never seen
life from the sky.

The butterfly remembers
where they've been.
Drinking turtle tears with salt
before they fly.

- A lesson from Dr. Latonya -

Dearest friend,

Do you recall a time when you've felt invisible? How did you manage that feeling?

_____
_____
_____
_____
_____
_____
_____
_____
_____
_____
_____
_____
_____
_____
_____
_____
_____
_____

Sometimes you see less when you are seen. Being invisible magnifies who's on your team.

- A lesson from Dr. Latonya -

Dearest friend,

    Please share some of your most fun experiences. What part of the fun did you enjoy most? How did you feel?

_____
_____
_____
_____
_____
_____
_____
_____
_____
_____
_____
_____
_____
_____
_____
_____

Live life!
Don't watch it go by.

Life is like the ocean. It can present peace, danger, fun, despair, healing, hurt, beauty or horror. You cannot control what it brings, but you can manage how it impacts you.

AUTHOR'S NOTE

    The years 2010-2021 were the most interesting years of my life. For years, I could not find the words to express my feelings. My feelings were buried by trauma.

    I was often asked, "How are you? Are you okay?" I typically responded with, "I'm okay". I was alive, functioning and slept fine. But those were the only words I was able to use to describe my feelings in the moment. I was not interested in false concerns and having my raw feelings disregarded.

It is many years later and "how I feel" has new meaning. I have lost best friends, loved ones and I had to get to the point where I refused to lose me. But, to get to me, I had to be willing to taste salt and shed the weight of my tears.

www.ingramcontent.com/pod-product-compliance
Lightning Source LLC
Chambersburg PA
CBHW072202160426
43197CB00012B/2495